TEACHER EDITION

# The Bear Went Over the Mountain

By
John Jacobson
and John Higgins

A M... EY OF
FRIENDSH... ENTURE

## Table of Contents

## Musical Performance Rights

# HAL•LEONARD®
## CORPORATION

7777 W. BLUEMOUND RD. P.O. BOX 13819 MILWAUKEE, WI 53213

Visit Hal Leonard Online at
www.halleonard.com

# Production Guide
*By John Jacobson*

# Introduction

We are all well acquainted with the simple tale of the bear that went over the mountain to get a new perspective on the world. We also know that, when he got to the top of it, all that he could see was "the other side of the mountain." Well, new research has uncovered the fact that there is actually a lot more to this story than one bear's rather anti-climatic trip to the top of a hill. Indeed, there are plenty of sub-plots that serve to teach Da Bear, his friends, cast members and audience alike that life is often more about the journey than the destination. Like in much of teaching, it's the getting there that really counts. In this little musical, big lessons can be learned, and there is room for every critter in the choir to participate and benefit from involvement in this musical climb!

There are some simple staging suggestions throughout the teacher's score of this musical that you should feel free to use, adapt or ignore, as suits your needs. Here are a few more ideas that might stimulate your own creativity. As always, in our musicals we encourage you to make changes and additions to truly make it your own: Add characters, combine roles, add songs, leave things out; whatever makes it the best experience for you and your cast and crew. For instance, I can think of a certain Miley Cyrus song that might make a perfect encore for your presentation. Hint: It's "The Climb." "Climb Every Mountain" from Sound of Music would be another option.

# The Cast

The cast is all of the animals of the forest. We gave you quite a list, which you could expand or shrink if you need to. You can never have too many birds, bunnies and skunks. There are two groups, daytime animals and nighttime animals. All are friendly. Janet Edewaard has provided some wonderful costume suggestions to help you out.

Owl

Da Bear

**Animals of the Day** (with speaking parts; adapt as necessary)

| | | | |
|---|---|---|---|
| Fox | 4 Mice | 1 Woodchuck | 2 Quails |
| 5 Bunnies | 2 Bobcats | 1 Cardinal | 1 Bluebird |
| 2 Badgers | 3 Chipmunks | 2 Turkeys | 5 Squirrels |
| 2 Beavers | 2 Deer | 2 Ducks | |

**Animals of the Night** (with speaking parts; adapt as necessary)

| | | | |
|---|---|---|---|
| 4 Raccoons | 1 Skunk | 1 Opossum | 3 Bats |

Sun

Moon

# Costume Suggestions

*By Janet Edewaard*

The basic costume for the animals will be a sweat suit. If you cannot buy the color you need, buy white or grey and dye them. We are suggesting that the basic headdress for each animal costume be a "doo-rag." They can be found online very inexpensively and can be dyed to match the sweat suit. Ears should be cut out of felt and hot glued to the doo-rag.

The birds need to each wear a leotard with yellow tights. They can be purchased online. Since birds are small, use your smallest girls who won't mind being in something that is so form-fitting. A pair of shorts or a short skirt can be added for modesty. Bird legs are skinny (and from someone who has been called "bird legs" her entire life, let those little girls show off their skinny little legs!) The birds all need wings. Take one yard of a matching color chiffon and gather it down the middle. Attach a loop of elastic to one end of each side, so the girl can put it on her wrist. Attach the gathered section to the back of the costume.

Face painting is going to be a must in this production. So many of the animals will just look like kids in sweat suits, unless you add face paint. You can purchase real "face paint" or, I find that tempra paint works just as well. Get a couple of moms to help paint faces before the show. The paint comes off easily with baby wipes.

**OWL –** Yellow tights and a brown leotard. Add brown wings. Paint the child's face brown and paint yellow circles around the eyes.

**DA BEAR –** Brown sweat suit. He should be one of your largest students. He needs medium brown ears. Paint his face black with a large tan area around his nose and mouth.

**FOX –** Rust-colored sweat suit with short dog ears. Add a long tail out of matching felt. Paint on a brown nose.

**BUNNIES –** The bunnies can be several colors: white, tan or brown. Use long bunny ears and put an insert of pink in the ears. Add a short tail of white felt, covered in cotton balls. The face needs to have a pink nose and whiskers.

**BADGER –** Grey sweat suit. Paint the child's face grey with a white stripe down the nose and sides of the face. Add short black ears to the doo-rag.

**MICE –** Grey sweat suits. Put large circular ears on the doo-rag with a pink insert in the ear. Add a pink nose and whiskers to the mice. Add a long pink tail out of felt, stuffed with "poly-fill".

**BOBCAT –** Tan sweat suit with very sharp pointed ears. Give him some cat whiskers. No tail.

**CHIPMUNK –** Brown sweat suit with a long brown tail. Short rounded ears. White eyes on a brown face.

**DEER –** Brown sweat suit. Short ears and a short white tail.

**WOODCHUCK (groundhog) –** Tan sweat suit, tan face, small ears.

**CARDINAL –** Red body, red wings.

**TURKEY –** Brown body, brown wings. Add festive plumage.

**DUCKS –** Brown body, brown wings. Add colorful face paint, as in a mallard or wood duck.

**QUAILS –** Brown body, brown wings. Add white stripes on face.

**BLUEBIRDS –** blue body, blue wings.

**RACCOONS –** Grey sweat suit, short rounded ears. White face with black eyes, painted like a "Zorro" mask. Big tail.

**SKUNKS –** Black sweat suit, short rounded ears. Hot glue a piece of white felt on top of the doo-rag. Cut a piece of white felt to run down the back of costume and large tail.

**OPOSSUMS –** Grey sweat suit, white face. Long skinny pink tail out of felt.

**BATS –** Brown sweat suit, short wings and a set of brown wing.

# The Set

The musical takes place in the forest that covers the famous mountain. You might decorate with trees, logs, rocks, plants and so on. The mountain could be your backdrop and could be as simple as a drawing on flats. You could also project a mountain picture if you have a scrim. Or, encourage your audience and cast to use their imagination and have no mountain at all. If you live near a mountain or a hill that your audience is familiar with, you might even personalize your show by using the actual name of that local landmark.

# The Show

Let's go through the show scene-by-scene and song-by-song.

### Opening

The musical opens with the wise owl speaking directly to the audience. This could be performed in front of a curtain if you have one, or in a spotlight as though the rest of the forest is still in the darkness of night. This is a relatively long piece of dialog, so you might have one of your older students or even a teacher play the owl. The owl plays an important role in the beginning and near the end of the show to summarize the moral of the story, so you want it to be heard and understood. It might be fun to have the owl on a perch in front of the audience even as they are arriving prior to the show. He could even recite wise sayings as people are taking their seats. Ben Franklin, Confucius, Einstein quotes would come to mind.

### Song 1: Good Morning

As the curtain opens or the lights come slowly up, the forest is just waking up to a new day. It is a gentle opening, the way we all like to wake up. The animals arise a few at a time, stretching, yawning, waving to each other or shaking hands. Since it ends up being a round, you could have two obviously different groups singing. You might even have the two groups be the daytime and nighttime animals. As the daytime animals are waking up, the nighttime animals might pretend to be finding a nice place to sleep.

The lights could get brighter as the song continues. You might even begin with one child who plays the moon and another the sun. As the song progresses, the moon disappears and the sun takes over.

## Scene 1

In this scene, the first few characters speak directly to the audience. Da Bear makes his first appearance from behind a log or rock. Then the dialog proceeds between characters. Probably, one of the older (bigger) kids should play the bear as a focal point, but with good acting, any size will do. He is grumpy in a cute way, like someone just waking up.

## Song 2: This Is the Day

This is a song about determination. It is the first high-energy song of the musical so it serves as a good start for the journey to follow. For extra business, you might have some of the critters packing suitcases, rucksacks and backpacks as though getting ready for a trip. The squirrels could be packing bags of nuts, the skunk packing deodorant, and so on. The end of the song excites even those that were very excited about taking off on this new adventure.

## Scene 2

During this scene, you might have those who are not doing the dialog, walking in place quietly behind the speakers as though the hike is progressing. Remember, you are hiking up hill and the forest floor is soft. You don't want to cover up the dialog with noisy feet.

## Song 3: Sing Your Own Song

You might notice that the melody in Song 3 is the same melody as Song 2, but with a different musical "feel." This should make teaching notes twice as easy. There is a short break in the middle when every animal is supposed to sing like the creature they are. There are a number of ways to do this. One would be for everyone to "sing" at the same time for a general cacophony of sound. It does not have to be a contest for volume. In fact, everyone should try their best to blend into the group so that all voices can be heard. Another choice is to come up with a cute rhythmic pattern of animals taking turns showing off their voice. For instance, you could do four bird chirps, followed by a bear growl, followed by an owl hoot and a coyote howl. Your cast might have a fun time coming up with this sort of pattern. When the song resumes, some of the animals could even keep this ostinato going as accompaniment to the rest of the song.

## Scene 3

During this scene, the cast is still walking but getting very tired. They should greatly overact. Also, it would be good if the scene could get gradually darker, as though the sun is setting. The "moon" character could reappear and the "sun" disappear.

## Song 4: Beware!

In the choreography notes, we suggest that you have flashlights that look like eyes peering out of the darkness. Two flashlights per character would make them look like eyes. If this doesn't work for your situation, you could simply have the nighttime animals creep out a few at a time and move amongst the daytime animals. They could even make their way through the audience. It is supposed to be frightening in only the cutest way.

You could add paper bats on doweling rods, gobos of flying creatures, black curtains to make things darker, and so on.

## Scene 4

We discover that the nighttime animals are nothing to be afraid of. They could still have a bit of a streetwise attitude. The dialog abandons the rhyming patterns of the rest of the show to show that things seem and sound different in the middle of the night. The nighttime animals easily laugh at themselves and are soon recognized as a friendly part of the forest.

You can include a short reprise of "This is the Day," but it is quickly halted as Da Bear is too exhausted to continue.

## Song 5: Push!

This rap song is supposed to help get Da Bear to the top of the hill. You can make a lot of this song solos if you choose or have everybody rap everything. Da Bear should get to one side of the stage. As the song progresses, you could have different characters, one or two at a time, get behind and pretend to push Da Bear up the mountain with no success. He doesn't budge. But as we get nearer to the end of the song, many of the cast members could get behind Da Bear and pretend to push on him and on each other. He moves and ends up center stage.

Another fun way to present this and only a bit more complicated is this. Behind the cast (upstage), rig up a footlight that shines from near the floor up onto the back wall of the stage. With the other stagelights dimmed or off, shine the light on Da Bear or an outline of a bear, so that his shadow is seen, bigger than life, on the back wall. Now add to the silhouette, more animal shadows that appear to be pushing Da Bear up the hill. By the end of the song, the shadows will move out of the footlight as though Da Bear progressed up the hill. He will then return to the middle of the stage as the lights come on and the song ends. This really is not as hard as it sounds. Try it with even just a big flashlight as your footlight to get an idea of how it works.

## Scene 5

All are elated that they have made it to the top of the mountain. Da Bear is back at center stage. The moon is gone; the sun is back. The lights are on. All are excited, except Da Bear who seems disappointed by the fact that all he sees is the other side of the mountain. This is an important scene as it summarizes the moral of the story.

## Song 6: Forever

A simple family portrait arrangement with Da Bear in the center would suffice for this song.

## Scene 6

Everyone is happy and changed forever.

### Reprise: This Is The Day/The Bear Went Over the Mountain

This is a chance for bows and to confirm the happy ending. You might have the skunk be the last one on stage for a bow, or as he walks out to take his bow, the rest of the cast hurries off stage. He shrugs and exits too.

# Conclusion

We hope you enjoy The Bear Went Over The Mountain. Teachers we hope we've made your monumental job a little easier. Cast members and parents we hope we've made your journey a bit more worthwhile.

## OPENING NARRATION

**Owl:** *(speaking to the audience)* Once upon a time, in a forest next to a hill, there lived a bear. The bear had many friends: squirrels, rabbits, bees, songbirds of every color, fox, deer and more. But he was restless. He felt there had to be more to life than raiding the hives of bees for their honey, eating berries and apples, and growing fatter and fatter until it was time to sleep again. He wanted to expand his horizons. So, he decided to climb to the top of the hill. Why? Well, you know that – "To see what he could see." At first, all of his friends tried to talk him out of it, but not me, Owl, who wisely advises him to go, explore, and learn.

# 1. Good Morning!

**Words and Music by JOHN JACOBSON and JOHN HIGGINS**

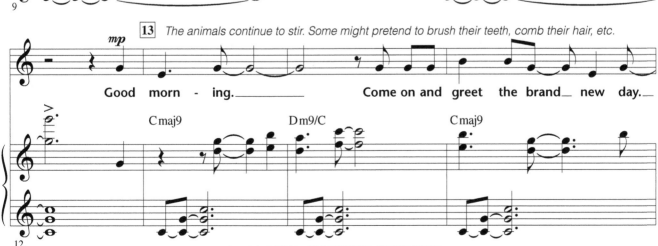

**STOP RECORDING**

## SCENE 1

*(When the song is over, the animals notice the audience and slowly start talking to them warily.)*

**Bunny 1:**            Good morning, you, whoever you are.
                        Welcome to our home.

**Bunny 2:**            This is our woods and the actual place
                        Where the deer and antelope roam.

**Badger 1:**           We all live here at the base of this hill,
                        Happily, all together.

**Beaver 1:**           Fox and squirrels, bunnies and bees
                        And many birds of a feather.

**Mouse 1:**            Look out! Look out! Da Bear is waking up.
                        He's been sleeping behind that stump.

**Mouse 2:**            When he wakes up from his winter nap,
                        He's always a terrible grump!

**Da Bear:**            *(waking up grumpily)*
                        Grr! Grr! Oh boy, what a nap!
                        I must have dozed off over there.
                        I feel like I've slept for months and months
                        And I'm as hungry as ... a bear!

*(All the other characters pretend to be very scared.)*

**Bobcat 1:**           Don't worry, Bear. It was only 10 weeks.
                        We're glad you are out of your den.
                        Now that your nap is over,
                        We celebrate spring again.

        **Da Bear:**        I'm tired of doing the same old thing,
                            Year after year after year.
                            I'd like to try something new for once.
                            I want to get out of here.

        **Chipmunk 1:**     Well, why don't you go on a little trip,
                            To shake off your hibernation?

| **Chipmunk 2:** | Yea! Da Bear, what you really need<br>Is a little spring vacation! |
|---|---|
| **Da Bear:** | Great idea! I know just where to go,<br>Up that mountain there.<br>I've always wanted to see the top<br>And breathe the mountain air. |

*(All are horrified by this idea.)*

| **Deer 1:** | Up that mountain? You can't be serious.<br>No one has ever gone there. |
|---|---|
| **Deer 2:** | It's not a good place to travel,<br>For a bunny, a hare or a bear. |
| **Da Bear:** | Well, I'm going. That's all there is to it.<br>Anyone can come along. |
| **Woodchuck:** | If we're going to climb that mountain,<br>We better sing a mountain song. |

## START RECORDING

# SONG 2: THIS IS THE DAY

# 2. This Is the Day

**Words and Music by JOHN JACOBSON
and JOHN HIGGINS**

*Lower hands and let go. Look at speaker, then react with high fives, clapping, hopping up and down, etc.*

**Speaker: "OK, I never thought I'd say this, but I'll go if all of you do!"**

**All:** *(ad lib)* **"All right!" "Now we're talkin'!" "Let's go!" etc.**

This is the day___ we're gon - na   climb  that  moun-tain.   This  is  the  day___ we're gon - na

make    our    way.    This   is   the  day___ we're gon - na    do      our  best,_  'cause

**STOP RECORDING**

## SCENE 2

**Cardinal:**                Oh, this hiking is so much fun.
But how do we know where to go?

**Turkey 1:**              Just keep hiking uphill, I guess.
Da Bear always seems to know.

**Duck 1:**                There are so many things to see on this trip,
So much to see and do.

**Duck 2:**                Whenever you travel out of your box,
Great things can happen to you.

**Quail 1:**               As long as we all stay together,
I guess we can't go wrong.

**Quail 2:**               And look, here are the birds and the bees
To sing a traveling song.

**START RECORDING**

# SONG 3: SING YOUR OWN SONG

# 3. Sing Your Own Song

Words and Music by JOHN JACOBSON
and JOHN HIGGINS

Easy shuffle (♩ = 108)

Piano

5 Walk in place, 2 steps per measure

Step by step, we trav-el off to-geth-er.

Stop walking. Reach to a small group of squirrels and bunnies who scurry around themselves in a circle.

One by one, come on, "a-way we go!" Some of us can scoot a-

Reach to the turtle, or another slow animal who takes one slow step.

round so quick-ly, some of us plod stead-y and slow.

*Animals take turns "sounding off" with their indigenous voices, and acting their part. See Production Guide for ideas.*

**33** *Walk in place*

Keep it up,__ we like the way you sound__ now. All to-geth - er when we sing out strong.

**STOP RECORDING**

## SCENE 3

*(All of the animals are getting a little tired.)*

**Bunny 3:**     My, oh my! It's been uphill all day.
My legs are starting to tire.

**Bunny 4:**     *(gasping)*
Mine, too, and to tell the truth,
My lungs are nearly on fire.

**Turkey 2:**     Now it's starting to get quite dark.
I'm seeing eyes everywhere.

**Badger 2:**     I feel like we're being followed.
Everyone better beware.

**Beaver 2:**     Look! I saw something moving,
Over there! And there! And there!

**Bobcat 2:**     The creatures of the night
Will catch you unaware!

*(All of the nocturnal animals enter and move among the daytime animals. There could be raccoons, skunks, opossums, bats, etc.)*

**START RECORDING**

# SONG 4: BEWARE!

# 4. Beware!

**Words and Music by JOHN JACOBSON
and JOHN HIGGINS**

*If possible, dim the lights. Night time animals each have two little flashlights that
they hold up like eyes shining in the dark. Take turns turning them on.*

**STOP RECORDING**

## SCENE 4

**Raccoon 1:**    Yo! Dudes! What's happening?

**Raccoon 2:**    Yeah, wassup?

**Day Animals:**    Ahhh!!

**Raccoon 3:**    *(to the bunny)* Whoa, 'little jumpy, aren't you? Get it, jumpy? *(laughs at his own joke)*

**Bunny 5:**    Ahh! Don't eat me! Please don't eat me. I have baby bunnies at home. Lots of them!!

**Raccoon 3:**    Eat you? Why would I eat you?

**Bunny 5:**    Because you're scary animals of the night, and that's what scary animals of the night do!

**Raccoon 4:**    You guys have been watching too many movies. We're not out to hurt anybody. We just see better at night. That's why we move around then.

**Bat 1:**    Me? I'm as blind as a bat. In fact, I am a bat! I move around at night because there's less traffic in the air.

**Bat 2:**    Yeah. We won't hurt you, unless, of course, you're a mosquito. We love mosquitoes.

**All Bats:**    Yummm!

**Squirrel 1:**    You mean, you night animals are friendly?

**Skunk:**    Sure! *(Everyone backs away from the skunk.)*

**Bat 3:**    Now, where are you all going?

**Fox:**    Well, Da Bear, there, wanted to go over the top of the mountain, so we decided to go along with him.

**Opossum:**    Cool! Can we come too?

**Mouse 3:**     Sure! Why not?

**All:**     Let's go!

*(Cast sings a short a cappella Reprise of "Sing Your Own Song" as the animals all start walking in place.)*

*(Da Bear interrupts them and they stop singing.)*

**Da Bear:**     *(exhausted)*
Stop! Stop! I can't go on.
I'm tired as a bear can be.
You can go up that mountain,
But you'll have to go without me.

**Cardinal:**     But wait, Da Bear! We're almost there.
We can't let you stop here!

**Bluebird:**     That's right! I can see the mountaintop.
The top is very near!

**Quail 1:**     Come on! We'll help.
You're not alone any more.
We'll help you reach the top,
'Cause that's what friends are for.

**Deer 1:**     Come on, everyone!
Get a hold and let's push!

## START RECORDING

# SONG 5: PUSH!

# 5. Push!

**Words and Music by JOHN JACOBSON
and JOHN HIGGINS**

*Do favorite rap moves during introduction.*
*Some will be pushing on Da Bear, while others do this choreography.*

**Forceful rap** (♩ = 100)

*Push both hands as if shoving something*

*Point to Da Bear*

*Repeat 2 measures*

Push, push! Our friend needs help, so push! Push, push! Our

*Punch air with fist on each letter*

*Hand down*

friend needs help, so push! P - U - S - H, ev - 'ry - bod - y push!

*Repeat 2 measures*

*Show muscles to the audience*

P - U - S - H, come on, y'all,_ let's push!

**STOP RECORDING**

**SCENE 5**

**Mouse 4:**    We made it! We made it! We reached the top!
We're as high as we can go.

**Chipmunk 3:**    Look! The sky is up above us,
And the clouds are down below.

**Squirrel 2:**    What is it, Bear? You look so blue.
What is making you so sad?

**Squirrel 3:**    You should be so happy!
You should be so glad.

**Da Bear:**    I'm looking over the mountain
But all that I can see,
Is the other side of the mountain,
And it looks the same to me.

**Owl:**    Now listen, Bear, and listen close.
I mean no disrespect.
But what in the world were you thinking?
What did you expect?

**Squirrel 4:**    Did you think it would be different,
That the world would be new and strange?

**Squirrel 5:**    Did you think when you climbed the mountain,
That everything would change?

**Da Bear:**    Yeah. Something like that.

**Owl:**
What a hoot, you silly bear!
Ever since you came,
It's very clear to all of us
That nothing is the same.

**Da Bear:**
Really?

**Owl:**
You see, it's not the end of the trip
That made you who you are.
It's the trip itself and all your friends
That took you oh, so far.

**Fox:**
We know each other better,
And no matter how it ends,
This journey made us smarter
And made us better friends.

**START RECORDING**

# SONG 6: FOREVER

# 6. Forever

**Words and Music by JOHN JACOBSON
and JOHN HIGGINS**

*Make a nice family portrait with Da Bear in the middle.*

**STOP RECORDING**

**SCENE 6**

**Da Bear:**        Thank you, everybody.
                    I think that I can see
                    That this trip I made with all of you,
                    Has made a better me!

**Fox:**            Next time you have a dream,
                    Just give us all a yelp.
                    You have all kinds of friends now,
                    And we'll be there to help!

**Da Bear:**        What a wonderful adventure.
                    You made it fun to roam.
                    I made it up the mountain.

**Skunk:**          Now let's all go home!

**START RECORDING**

# REPRISE: THIS IS THE DAY/THE BEAR WENT OVER THE MOUNTAIN

# Reprise: This Is the Day
## (with "The Bear Went Over the Mountain")

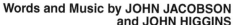
Words and Music by JOHN JACOBSON
and JOHN HIGGINS

*Lower hands and let go. Look at speaker, then react with high fives, clapping, hopping up and down, etc.*

**Speaker: "Well, Da Bear was right about journeys. Let's make another soon!"**

**All:** *(ad lib)* **"All right!" "Now we're talkin'!" "Let's go!" etc.**

Melody 2

The

*Da Bear walks around the stage and maybe even into the audience, shaking everyone's hand, giving high fives, recieving pats on the back. He can even say things like "Thanks for all the help," "That was GRRRRRReat!" and so on.*

**Melody 2**

bear went o - ver the moun - tain. The

**Melody 1** *Fists on hips*

*Point over audience*

This is the day___ we're gon - na climb that moun - tain.

**TEACHING OBJECTIVES AND NATIONAL STANDARDS FOR**

# The Bear Went Over the Mountain

The complete National Arts Standards and additional materials relating to the Standards are available from MENC: **www.menc.org**.

## Objectives for Good Morning!

- Sing in tune and maintain steady beat
- Sing a song with 2 parts and maintain pitch and steady beat
- Identify and locate so and mi in a song
- Read and perform *mp, mf, cresc, dim, accent* and *fermata*

*This lesson addresses the National Standards for Music **K–4** Education: 1b, 1d, 1e, 5b. 5c, 6b, 6e.*

_____

## Objectives for This Is the Day

- Sing in tune and maintain steady beat
- Sing a song with 2 parts and maintain pitch and steady beat
- Identify repeated motives
- Identify and perform *crescendo, mf, f, ff*
- Identify and locate a key change

*This lesson addresses the National Standards for Music **K–4** Education: 1d, 1e, 5c, 6b, 6c.*

_____

## Objectives for Sing Your Own Song

- Sing in tune and maintain steady beat
- Sing a song with 2 parts and maintain pitch and steady beat
- Discuss the effect tempo changes have on a piece of music
- Identify repeated motives
- Improvise animal sounds use body or vocal sounds

*This lesson addresses the National Standards for Music **K–4** Education: 1b, 1d, 1e, 3d, 6c, 6e, 9c.*

_____

## Objectives for Beware!

- Sing in tune and maintain steady beat
- Sing a song with 2 parts and maintain pitch and steady beat
- Discuss characteristics of a minor song
- Read and perform syncopation
- Locate a scale fragment
- Read and perform *mf, f, ff, cresc, accent*

*This lesson addresses the National Standards for Music **K–4** Education: 1b, 1d, 1e, 5a, 5b, 5c, 6b, 6c.*

_____

## Objectives for Push!

• Compare and contrast singing with rapping (speaking vs. singing voice)
• Identify repeated measures
• Identify solo and unison voices
• Compare and contrast the style of rap music with music of other cultures

*This lesson addresses the National Standards for Music* **K—4** *Education: 6b, 6c, 6e, 7b, 9a.*

---

## Objectives for Forever

• Sing in tune and maintain steady beat
• Read and perform syncopation
• Locate repeated melodic fragments
• Read and perform *mp, mf, f, cresc, accent*

*This lesson addresses the National Standards for Music* **K—4** *Education: 1b, 1e, 5a, 5b, 5c, 6b, 6c, 6e, 9e.*

---

## Objectives for Reprise: This Is the Day

• Sing in tune and maintain steady beat
• Sing a song with 2 parts and maintain pitch and steady beat
• Identify repeated and contrasting sections
• Identify and perform *crescendo, mf, f, ff*
• Identify and locate a key change

*This lesson addresses the National Standards for Music* **K—4** *Education: 1d, 1e, 5c, 6a, 6b, 6c.*

# The Bear Went Over the Mountain

## Went Over the

## Mountain

By
John Jacobson
and John Higgins

### A MUSICAL JOURNEY OF FRIENDSHIP & ADVENTURE

ExpressiveArts®

HAL•LEONARD®

# Teacher's Notes

# About the Writers

In October of 2001 President George Bush named **JOHN JACOBSON** a Point of Light award winner for his "dedication to providing young people involved in the arts opportunities to combine music, charitable giving and community service." John is the founder and volunteer president of America Sings! Inc., a non-profit organization that encourages young performers to use their time and talents for community service. With a bachelor's degree in Music Education from the University of Wisconsin-Madison and a Master's Degree in Liberal Studies from Georgetown University, John is recognized internationally as a creative and motivating speaker for teachers and students involved in choral music education. He is the author and composer of many musicals and choral works that have been performed by millions of children worldwide, as well as educational videos and tapes that have helped music educators excel in their individual teaching arenas, all published exclusively by Hal Leonard Corporation. John has staged hundreds of huge music festival ensembles in his association with Walt Disney Productions and directed productions featuring thousands of young singers including NBC's national broadcast of the Macy's Thanksgiving Day Parade, presidential inaugurations and more. John stars in children's musical and exercise videotapes, most recently the series *Jjump! A Fitness Program for Children* and is the Senior Contributing Writer for *John Jacobson's Music Express*, an educational magazine for young children published by Hal Leonard Corporation.

**JOHN HIGGINS** is Managing Producer/Editor for Hal Leonard Corporation. A co-author in the Essential Elements series of methods, John is best known for his many compositions and arrangements for choirs, bands and orchestras. As a composer of children's songs, he has collaborated with notables like John Jacobson, Roger Emerson and Emily Crocker on musicals such as *How Does Your Garden Grow? Bugz, The Littlest Reindeer* and *A Storybook Christmas*. John has also arranged and produced a large catalog of children's music, including *The Runaway Snowman, Peace Child*, and Leslie Bricusse's *Scrooge*. His recording production for McGraw-Hill's *Share The Music* textbook series included music from *Sesame Street*, *Disney* films and a special project with the late Fred Rogers of *Mr. Rogers' Neighborhood*. In two series of Broadway shows for young performers, John arranged and produced new versions of *Annie, Guys & Dolls, Fiddler On The Roof, The King And I*, and *The Music Man*. His two Grammy award-winning projects include arranging on Sandi Patti's *Another Time, Another Place* (Best Pop Gospel Album) and co-producing on Rob McConnell's *Live in Digital* (Best Big Band Jazz Album). He orchestrated and conducted the music for the stage premiere of *Willy Wonka* at the Kennedy Center in Washington, D.C. John served as president of Jenson Publications before it became a part of the Hal Leonard Corporation. In addition to his writing and producing activities, he maintains a role in music education as a guest-conductor, clinician and author.